PICK UP THE PHONE

FUNDAMENTALS OF MODERN TELEMARKETING

By Chris Jackson

This book is written by a seasoned professional and serves as a guide for those who are starting out in the world of telemarketing, or those who want to learn how to run a successful project from start to completion, and for those who are looking for better ways to retain staff in an industry that has a high turn-over.

Each chapter will look at the different styles of telemarketing, and how you can make the most of your hiring efforts in a changing world.

To make contact with the writer for bookings, appearances, write to:

Chris Jackson

leadsnz@yahoo.com

© 2009 Chris Jackson

ISBN 978-1-4092-8273-0

Table of Contents

FOREWORD

My experience in the industry spans the last 15 years and I have had the pleasure of working with some of the most talented people in the business. My experience in the industry has covered every aspect of call center operations, from being a part time telesales person to training and recruiting call center staff.

Sadly, telemarketing has been branded as the worst of all jobs, but as I will explain in a later chapter, telemarketing is the backbone of every business, whether you are a start-up or Fortune 50 company.

My career in telemarketing happened quite by accident. It was 1994 and at the time I was living in a suburb of Brisbane, Australia. In 1994 I had just come out of the nursing industry and I wanted a change of direction. So when I was offered a part time position at a finance company, my feelings on the new job were mixed, as my understanding of the industry was naïve at best.

In mid 1994 I started working for an insurance company that specialized in a variety of policies, but none so much as popular as their Education Savings Plan and their Funeral Plans. My job was to call a list of potential prospects and set an appointment for one of the many sales agents to give an obligation free consultation. Of course, that was a lot easier than it sounded, but at the time I did think it would be an easy task. Not so as I found out.

I worked for that small insurance firm for some months, starting on a part time basis, and then working full time. In the time I worked there I successfully managed to keep 7 sales agents fully booked, 5 days a week. On any given week I was booking 60 to 100 appointments a week, every week. Cold calling was never easy, especially calling residential listings. But I liked the job and I got to meet a variety of people, even if it meant that I was meeting them just over the phone.

* * * *

One of the first lessons I learned early on was *"Don't Sound like a Telemarketer."* Sure, it can be easy to read a script, and even these days I hear it so often from telemarketers. They sit and read a script to the prospect and read it verbatim and sound like a robot! No wonder prospects tell them no! I will explain more about this topic in another chapter, and how you can overcome the common mistake of sounding robotic.

Another point that is important to remember is the "*Art Of Dealing With Rejection*". Rejection is not an easy thing to overcome, as no-one likes to be rejected, whether it is in work, pleasure or otherwise. But as I learned, and you should learn, when a prospect says No, that is not giving you a rejection. They are rejecting the proposal or offer presented, and naturally, just because the prospect says No now, does not mean that they will have the same mind-set in 3 week or 3 months from now. In most cases, a prospect will say No because it does not fit their current methodologies, their budget or they simply do not have the genuine time to look at what is being offered. If you run a business you will know what I am talking about. I will explain more about this topic in the chapter *The Art Of Dealing With Rejection*.

* * * *

I can remember the days before the internet became popular. Now for you X-Geners, this may seem like a hard concept to grasp. But when I started out in telemarketing, the thought of using an online CRM or "googling" a company was about as remote as home computers were back in the 1970's.

Back in the early 90's, unless a business had their own data, it was commonplace for data companies to "sell" such lists of residential and business listings. Quite often that data would be incorrect as it was gathered by using the current records from the Yellow and White Pages.

Many business owners I worked with in the early days purchased lists from companies such as OzOnDisc. And as far as I recall, that was one of the most reliable sources in Australia to purchase from. Times have certainly changed since those early days.

Welcome 21st century technology! Today, even though there are reputable companies on the internet such as InfoUSA and Hoovers – where you can purchase the most up to date records of companies – still many small businesses will opt to search through their local yellow pages (either online or book) for prospects in their regional area. Data – accurate data – is the essential foundation of a thriving business. It is a means to introduce your product or service to other business people in your community, and unless you are a well known corporation, if you own a business in the average city of more than 100,000 people, it is unlikely that prospects will even know you exist. So what does work in today's ever changing market? The Internet? Flyers? Traditional advertising in your local newspaper? I will explore these options more in the chapter *Traditional Marketing For Today*.

Now since I am on the topic of traditions in the 21st century, I will explain a little how telecommuting has changed over the years and how it affects ever changing businesses. Telecommuting started around 1990 when they Clean Air Acts Amendment was introduced. The Amendment required the America's most polluted regions to reduce the number of single-occupant vehicles by up to 13%. Soon afterward, companies began experimenting with telecommuting programs as a way to reduce employee turnover, thereby reducing the high cost of recruiting and training new employees.

Over the years, telecommuting advocates have heralded technology as a means for transforming the way we do business. Now that broadband services such as DSL and cable modems are widely available -- making it easier for off-site employees to stay in touch -- telecommuting is experiencing its second wave. Telecommuting has become a feasible option for a number of companies, large and small. As a result there has been a wave of telemarketers who will search for jobs where they can work from home.

There is a definite advantage of working from home. No commute in traffic, less stress, familiarity with your environment and if you have Time Management skills, it allows you to successfully balance home life with work life. If you don't have Time Management skills, you need to learn the basics of what this means in the chapter *Time Management: How To Balance Work & Personal Time*.

Although there are advantages for both the employer and contractor, there are also the negative aspects such as high retention rate, unwillingness to work, no supervision, lack of ethics and moral by freelance consultants. Although it cannot be said for those who do actually work, I have personally seen a steady decline in the ethics and moral of Work At Home Telemarketers over the years. For one reason or another the diligence and ethic has been thrown out the window for the hope of getting an easy paycheck or thinking that all work at home opportunities are too good to be true.

If you are a freelancer or want to explore the possibility of working from home, then you do need to understand what it means to *Work From Home*, as I will explain in the chapter *So You Want To Work From Home*.

It is true that with the wave of the internet boom, there are dozens – even hundreds – of work at home scams. You see them every day with titles such as "*Earn $1000 this week!*" and "*Last Year I earned $100,000 by working from home*". Such ads you will see all the time on directories such as Gumtree and Craigslist. These headlines often attract the naïve by offering a get-rich-quick promise, but as I will point out in *Modern Scams*, these are headlines – offers - that you should be aware of. Any reputable employer will not ask you for a fee to work from home. If any employer does, you know that it is a scam, and all you will get in return is a loss of your cash. This chapter will tell you what to look for in job offerings, as well as the best places online to find reputable work offers.

* * * *

In recent years, there has also been a trend in Outsourcing. Like the Work From Home opportunities that exist in the marketplace, Outsourcing has become a viable and affordable means to outsource to call centers in third world countries such as India, Pakistan, China, Singapore and the Philippines. Being cost-effective for many companies – such as banks, government departments, and most other places where you call a toll free customer service number – means finding a solution that otherwise fits the growing demands of a corporation. Outsourcing an Inbound project to call centers offshore means little or no overheads, no ongoing recruiting and lastly, the project gets fulfilled.

While this has proven to be viable for a lot of Inbound campaigns, with the promise of cheap labor as low as $2US an hour in some call centers, outsourcing an Outbound project does not always prove profitable, especially if you own a business in North America and you want to target prospects in your region. The willingness of call centers in third world countries is there, and it is true that if you get a good call center offshore the results can be great, but more often than not, leads – your leads – are wasted because a majority of call center staff in developing countries will speak English as a second or third language, and the message conveyed to your prospect can be lost.

If you are a business what options do you have in the ever changing world? Hire an in-house staff? Outsource to a developing country or take a chance of Work At Home people, who actually may not work from home. There are advantages and disadvantages to all three options. But I will look at those options in the chapter *Business Making Business*.

* * * *

The bottom line in any call center project is you want results. When you start a call center it is in your business plan to succeed and have the best agents working for you. But finding the best agents is not an easy process. There is the time taken to place advertisements, the costs associated with advertising, recruiting personnel, interview and screening process, then hiring the individual(s). telemarketing has a high industry turn-over. In fact, one of the highest in any industry. As an employer what can you do to have less turnover and loyal staff? I will look at your options as a call center in the chapter *Getting The Most For Your Buck*. I will also look at *Telemarketing Tips*.

Chapter One –

History Of Telemarketing

Telemarketing. Love it or hate it, it is still the hub in all types of businesses. Whether you realize it or not, even the average person who has never worked in a call center has done telemarketing in one form or another.

Let me explain: When you call a mechanic or a carpenter for a quote, you don't call just one business and settle for whatever price they give you on the phone. No, if you are savvy you will call several businesses and shop around for the best quote. That, my friend, is telemarketing.

When you call a removalist, do you go with the first one you call or call several? Again, if you are savvy you will call several and find out the best service for the best price. That is telemarketing.

When you are looking to sell your house, do you call one real estate or several? Again, telemarketing.

When you want to go to a nice resort for a weekend do you go to the first one that comes to mind or do you call several and find out their availability and rates? Again – telemarketing.

Whether you are a consumer or a business, telemarketing is something we all do at one time or another. Whether you are John Q. Taxpayer or a seasoned professional you know what telemarketing is.

Telemarketing – as I have explained – is the life-blood of every business in the modern world. It allows businesses to communicate their product or service to consumers rapidly and sometimes cost effectively.

Yet telemarketing wasn't always so easy. Telemarketing – it is believed – started in the 1960's when [1]Murray Roman opened a store in Manhattan and called it Campaign Communications, where he hired out of work actors to put some feeling into selling subscriptions for Saturday Review. By the early 1970's, telemarketing had spread across the country, but there were no advanced technologies, no market research, no training programs, no scripts.

As enterprising as Murray was, it is believed that telemarketing began much earlier, in the 1930's. R.R. Donnelley in 1930 pioneered telemarketing by using it to entice advertisers to buy ad space for the Business Yellow Pages. This opened the door for using the telephone for business, and in turn, was the birth of a great industry.

---

[1] http://www.washingtonpost.com/ac2/wp-dyn/A45989-2002Oct18?language=printer

During the 1970's most companies just had a bank of rotary telephones and stacks of 3-by-5 cards with names and numbers straight out of the phone book. The concept was simply making a person-to-person sales connection over the phone.

Then technology changed. Telemarketing turned ugly and started to get a bad reputation.

By the mid 1980's, predictive dialing -- automated speed dialing to multiple customers simultaneously -- was making telemarketing more efficient but also impersonal and maddening, leaving all but the first customers to pick up the phone hearing a click.

Anticipating a backlash, in 1985 the Direct Marketing Association, a trade association representing all direct marketers, from telemarketers to junk-mailers, created a "telephone preference service" supposedly enabling people to opt out of telemarketer calls from its member companies. But the problem persisted.

In 1991, Congress passed the Telephone Consumer Protection Act, granting consumers certain rights to defend themselves against telemarketing. In 1995, the Telemarketing Sales Rule targeted deceptive and abusive telemarketing practices.

But the problem grew to mega-monster proportions.

A cheap and effective method of selling (the industry estimates roughly $3.50 in sales for every dollar spent), telemarketing ranked fourth of the 100 Worst Ideas of the 20th Century, according to a Time Magazine poll.

In recent years, telemarketing has received many a back-lash and over the top regulations. The United States, Australia, Canada, the UK, all have national Do Not Call registries, as I will show in the following examples.

Although DNC Registries were implemented to stop the barrage of over-calls by some telemarketing firms, some regulations imposed have been seen and viewed as over-enforcement.

* * * *

In the United States, the Federal Trade Commission (FTC) [2] opened the National Do Not Call Registry in June 2003 to comply with the Do-Not-Call Implementation Act. According to the 2009 Economic Report of the President, prepared by the Council of Economic Advisors:

> The program has proved quite popular: as of 2007, according to one survey, 72 percent of Americans had registered on the list, and 77 percent of those say that

---

[2] http://en.wikipedia.org/wiki/United_States_National_Do_Not_Call_Registry

it made a large difference in the number of telemarketing calls that they receive (another 14 percent report a small reduction in calls). Another survey, conducted less than a year after the Do Not Call list was implemented, found that people who registered for the list saw a reduction in telemarketing calls from an average of 30 calls per month to an average of 6 per month.

However, according to the report on the FTC website dated April 2008: Telephone numbers placed on the National Do Not Call Registry will remain on it permanently due to the Do-Not-Call Improvement Act of 2007, which became law in February 2008. More than 157 million phone numbers are on the National Do Not Call Registry.[3]

Placing your number on the U.S. National Do Not Call Registry will stop most unsolicited calls. In the United States, the following are exceptions granted by existing laws and regulations.

- ✓ The registry only applies to residential lines, not to business lines.
- ✓ A person may still receive calls from political organizations.
- ✓ A person may still receive calls from charities.
- ✓ A person may still receive calls from those conducting surveys.
- ✓ A person may still receive calls from companies with which he or she has an existing business relationship for up to 18 months after his or her last purchase, payment, or delivery from it, unless person specifically asks the company not to call again.
- ✓ A person may still receive calls from a company up to three months after submitting an application or inquiry to that company, unless the company is specifically asked not to call.
- ✓ A person may still receive calls from bill collectors (either primary creditors or collection agencies.). These callers are, however, regulated by other laws, such as those limiting them to calling during "reasonable hours." Some creditors may not call debtors who file for bankruptcy protection.

While a majority of residential households in the United States seem to opt to be on the DNC list, the Do Not Call Registry varies from country to country, as I will explain further.

* * * *

In Canada, the DNC Registry was first announced by the Canadian Government on December 13, 2004. It follows the model set by the National Do Not Call Registry established in the United States in June 2003.

---

[3] http://www.ftc.gov/opa/2008/04/dncfyi.shtm

The DNC list has been labeled a "disaster" and received heavy criticism due to both the large number of exempt groups and serious loopholes that allowed anyone to obtain the list.

On April 20, 2009, the Canadian Radio & Telecommunications Commission (CRTC) announced that telephone and fax numbers on the list would be protected from marketing calls for five years, extended from the three years at the list's inception.

As in the United States, registering on the National DNCL will not eliminate all telemarketing calls as there are some exemptions, including calls for or on behalf of: [4]

- ✓ Canadian registered charities;
- ✓ Organizations that you have done business with in the past eighteen (18) months, or to whom you have made an inquiry in the past six (6) months;
- ✓ Political parties, candidates, and associations of members of a political party;
- ✓ Persons collecting information for a survey of members of the public;
- ✓ Newspapers of general circulation for the purpose of soliciting subscriptions;
- ✓ Persons or entities to whom you have provided express consent to be called; or
- ✓ Calls to businesses.

* * * *

[5]Australia has a 'National Do Not Call Registry' to curb the growing amount telemarketing telephone calls that Australians receive. Legislation was passed in the Parliament of Australia on June 30, 2006 enacting the Do Not Call Register Act 2006. The Australian Communications and Media Authority is responsible for establishing and overseeing the register and has appointed Service Stream Solutions Pty Ltd to operate the Do Not Call Register.

The Do Not Call Register and the Industry Standard commenced on May 1st, 2007. On the first day it was inundated with traffic and apparently 'crashed' under the load.

The register has attracted some criticism for not attempting to curb unsolicited calls from charities and political parties.

- ✓ Charities
- ✓ Religious organizations
- ✓ Educational institutions
- ✓ Government bodies

---

[4] https://www.lnnte-dncl.gc.ca/dncla-adncl-eng
[5] http://en.wikipedia.org/wiki/Australian_Do_Not_Call_Register

✓ Registered political parties, independent MPs and political candidates

[6]A number of other types of calls are also not considered 'telemarketing' calls for the purposes of the Act, and may continue to be received. These are:

✓ product recall calls
✓ fault rectification calls
✓ appointment rescheduling calls
✓ appointment reminder calls
✓ calls relating to payments
✓ solicited calls
✓ one of the above call types that is not answered by the person to whom the call is made.

According to latest media releases on the ACMA website, approximately 2.3 million households are currently on the DNC Registry in Australia. [7]

* * * *

In the United Kingdom, The Telephone Preference Service (TPS) is an opt-out telephone list that is intended to prevent telemarketing calls to those who do not wish to receive them. The list is administered on behalf of Ofcom by the British direct marketing industry, who also run the Mailing Preference Service and Fax Preference Service. In 2005, the BBC reported that there were 10.5 million numbers registered. At the end of the year 2007, 14.8 million numbers were registered.

The TPS should not be confused with the Government Telephone Preference Scheme which refers exclusively to the system used by the General Post Office since 1952 and later BT to keep selected telephones operating during wartime when access to the telephone system by the general public would be denied.

The TPS only applies to cold calling: companies can still contact their own customers regardless of TPS to offer new products and services so long as the customer has not opted out from this with the individual company. Genuine market research is also allowed and calls from overseas made by overseas companies on their own account cannot be controlled by registering with the TPS. Individuals and businesses may opt-out on a case by case basis by objecting to these types of organizations directly.[8]

---

[6] http://www.acma.gov.au/WEB/STANDARD//pc=PC_310500
[7] http://www.acma.gov.au/WEB/STANDARD/pc=PC_311181
[8] http://www.tpsonline.org.uk/tps/

While it can be said that the regulations have been enforced across the board, the examples above show that these regulations do not apply for businesses. In today's market, if you are a business owner, you need to be able to reach out to a new audience.

It does seem that in order to thrive in the ever changing rules, many businesses are refocusing their efforts to a newer audience, such as the social network sites such as MySpace, Facebook and Twitter. These social networking avenues, while may gain exposure, do not always prove to be profitable. At best, they create a level of awareness of who you are, but without proper marketing in place, they serve no end of the challenge you are faced with.

Although there are strict rules in place with B2C telemarketing, the same cannot be said for B2B telemarketing. In today's world, a business needs to stay in touch with new prospects and opportunities. The effective way to do this is by knowing who your target market is.

The future of telemarketing from the standpoint of many does seem uncertain. But if you are going to survive in an ever changing world, a business needs to evolve and change with it.

Technology is changing how we conduct business. Gone are the days of index cards with hand-written customer data. Today we use sophisticated database tracking methods which can analyze, segment, and target specific markets. Large companies have established call centers with automatic dialing to reach their prospective customers. With corporate emphasis on becoming "lean and mean" and reducing costs, more and more companies are looking to experiment with telemarketing. No matter what your industry or size, you may be able to reap the benefits from using telemarketing in your integrated marketing strategy.

There is a saying which is true. *Those who adapt flourish. Those who do not perish.*

Chapter Two –

Types of Telemarketing

Unless you have been a telemarketer, you would have no idea what types of telemarketing there is. Telemarketing is more than calling homeowners at dinner time and pitching a subscription to the Post.

The telemarketing scope is a broad spectrum that encompasses not only the residential market (B2C) but the business market (B2B) also.

While it can be said that the B2C market does not have the wide playing field that B2B does, there is a certain allowance that needs to be given for those who call you on your home number at dinner time.

Let's look at the different types of telemarketing that fits the B2C and B2B marketplace:

In-bound Telemarketing:

Inbound Telemarketing is any call that is placed to a toll free number that you will see in catalogs, direct mail, emails, faxes, print ads, on websites and in TV/radio spots. Call centers will receive these calls, answer questions, and sell your product or service.

Outbound Telemarketing:

Warm or Cold Calling customers and prospects to sell products and services, generate and qualify leads, prompt them to visit stores and showrooms and set appointments. Your telemarketing call center can also notify current customers of special sales and promotions.

Business to Business Telemarketing:

Acquire new customers, qualify prospects and pass hot leads to sales reps and deal closers. Your telemarketing can keep other businesses aware of your latest products and services.

Business to Consumer Telemarketing:

Notify people who depend on your outbound telemarketing and inbound telemarketing programs to buy goods and services. Present special offers to prospects and existing customers with outbound telemarketing calls.

Telemarketing (or telesales) has proven effective for businesses of all types and sizes. Any of these types of telemarketing may be used separately, or in combination, to provide the optimum results for the sale of your product.

Charity and Fund Raising Telemarketing:

Calling attempts to raise both money and awareness for various charitable funds. If calls are made in-house, charity telemarketing calls are exempt from the Do Not Call Registry guidelines.

Customer Appreciation Telemarketing:

A call made solely to thank a customer for his or her loyal business is an example of customer appreciation telemarketing. These calls do not involve direct sales.

Database Clean-Up Telemarketing:

A process that is used to ensure a company's database of customer information is accurate often uses database clean-up. The call may verify such information as address, phone number, current account holder, account type and desired level of service.

Direct Sales Telemarketing:

When a telephone sales representative calls a number on a list and attempts to sell them a product over the phone s/he is engaging in direct sales telemarketing.

Get Out and Vote Telemarketing:

Calls aimed at motivating citizens to vote for a particular candidate are known as "get out and vote" telemarketing calls. If done in-house, "get out and vote" calls may be exempt from the Do Not Call Registry guidelines.

Lead Generating/Setting Telemarketing:

Lead generating is geared toward amassing sales leads for a particular company through telemarketing.

Market Research Telemarketing:

Calls done purely for research are exempt from the Do Not Call Registry guidelines. These calls attempt to gather accurate information about consumers and can be as broad or as specific as needed to research a certain market.

New Customer Acquisition Telemarketing:

Also known as "cold-calling" and involves a telephone sales representative calling a number on a list and soliciting business with no prior business relationship in place.

Renewal Telemarketing:

Calls made by telephone customer service representatives to check for a renewal of a subscription, service or memberships are renewal telemarketing calls.

Retention Telemarketing:

If a customer cancels a membership, subscription or services, a telephone sales representative will call and attempt to win back customer loyalty, engaging in retention telemarketing.

As the above examples point out, the telemarketing industry has a wide scope of focus. Whether you are a charitable organization or a small business that offers courier services. Telemarketing can enable your business to grow in your target audience.

Chapter Three –

Don't Sound like a Telemarketer

This is the most important lesson to learn in the art of telemarketing. *Don't sound like a telemarketer*!

Have you had a telemarketer call you, and instead of sounding like they know about the product or service, they sound like they are reading the script verbatim? If you have, then you know what I am talking about. Those type of telemarketers are robotic and often do not last long in the industry, although they do try hard. They find that they stumble on every sentence and get frustrated with the script and themselves very easily, and in the end quit.

Honestly, I have heard it and seen it too many times, and I have trained agents to becoming great sales people. In any lecture I give on telemarketing, my first rule is always *Don't Sound Like A Telemarketer*.

Over the years I have seen several types of Telemarketers. The type I can classify into the following categories:

- ✓ **Tele-Pro** – Otherwise known in some circles as *Sales Animals*. You know these types of people. They read a script once and they run with it. These types are flawless and have a sharp rebuttal for every objection thrown at them. These people are worth their weight in gold as not only are they born leaders, but they generate the results with minimal effort. Some Animals have the experience behind them, while others fit into this category with no prior experience. When I ran a call center in Ohio back in 2002, one such girl came to work for me and she took to telemarketing straight away. Kelly had no prior experience in the game, but from the first day she was on the phone she generated more results than the rest of the team. People like Kelly are the people you need as your leaders.

- ✓ **Tele-Novice** – These types of people are the ones that are satisfied in hitting their weekly quota or SPH and blending in with the rest of the team. They accredit their success to being a team-effort. While they have the understanding of Telemarketing Dynamics, they have no real reason or drive to stand out and make their mark as leaders. Although they know the scripts and rebuttals verbatim, they could achieve a lot more with proper direction and coaching.

- ✓ **Tele-Wannabe** – Okay, we all know these types. They try so hard to get the script right, but they stumble at every point and quite often do not last more than a few weeks. Although they may have a liking for the industry or the product/service, they require ongoing training to bring them up to speed to fit in with the rest of the team. It is unfortunate that a lot fit into this category, as I have seen it so many times in the call centers I have worked in and coached.

- ✓ **Tele-This-Weeker** – These types see telemarketing as a means to paying their bills for this week and the next and they have no real love for the industry. Unfortunately these types of people are a dime-a-dozen and can be hired with no effort and no amount of training will hold their attention more than 5 seconds as all that is on their mind is minimal work for easy pay. I have seen these types of people a lot. There are a lot of those ones on sites such as Guru, GetAFreelancer and Monster. While they claim in their resume that they have experience, they quite often do not and are better suited for a supervised position. Over the years, I have personally hired people from such sites, and the routine is always the same. Such people expect an hourly rate then do not follow company guidelines. Unfortunately, such people are not worth hiring as it will end up costing the employer time and money for no ROI. Now, this may offend some, but these things are true. Colleagues I have worked with over the years have said the same thing.

As I pointed out above, there are four categories of telemarketers. Now, you are not always going to get a Tele-Pro straight away as those types are like searching for a nugget of gold in a quarry filled with rubble. But quite often you will come across the Tele-Novice and the Tele-Wannabe's.

If you are a pro or a Novice, you can skip ahead to the next section as this is for the Wannabe's and the Try-Hard's.

What objections do you face when dealing with stumbling and sounding like you are reading the script? When a prospect gives you an objection do you have the rebuttal already in your mind or do you stammer for an answer until you find the rebuttal script?

The amount of times I have heard telemarketers stumble in this area is unbelievable. And the thing is, they don't realize that they are doing it. Now, I have worked with some call centers in the US and Australia where their team was like a well-oiled machine, the pitch and delivery absolutely perfect. But, with that in mind I have also seen call centers where the training methodologies are non-existent and the telemarketer is expected to know everything from the first day they are hired.

Bad idea!

Being a Telemarketer and sounding like a Telemarketer is two different breeds and for the Wannabe's you need to first ask yourself why you are in the industry to begin with? Are you doing it for the love of the game or because you want to pay the bills this week or both?

In order to succeed in Modern Telemarketing you need to learn the script. If necessary, take the script home with you and practice in the mirror. Watch yourself speak and repeat it over and over again. The only way you can get out of the rut of sounding like a telemarketer is *knowing the script*.

Over the years I have trained telemarketers how to deliver a script perfectly. Look at it from an actor's point of view. An actor will memorize their lines, their script, and they will give a performance in the endeavor to get a great review by movie critics. A telemarketing script, while on a different playing field, is similar. You are an actor, and you need to know your lines if you are going to be convincing enough to the buyer.

An actor will sell out to the script they are working on. Quite often you will read articles on how top ranking actors will gain so many pounds for one role, and then shed much more for another role. Such actors and actresses prime and get themselves into character. If the film is based on a true story, such notable actors and actresses will do their homework on the character and get into the mindset of delivering a pitch that is believable.

As a telemarketer you don't have to go through the long research and long hours as top actors and actresses do, but you do need to get into character and deliver a pitch that is believable.

You want to hit the top sales for this week but don't know how? Read the script. Read it, memorize it, know your lines, and believe in the product or service being offered. Know it in the way that if Customer X throws an unexpected objection at you, you have a sharp rebuttal already in mind.

That is how you succeed and how you stop sounding like a telemarketer.

Read, Know, Believe.

Chapter Four –

The Art Of Dealing With Rejection

Not Interested! Those are the famous words you will hear more often than you will have hot dinners! How do you deal with rejection? Unless you are a trained professional, taking a rejection from a prospect is never easy.

In telemarketing, you have to become adaptable in hearing rejection. I see so many telemarketers fail at being telemarketers because they cannot handle a prospect telling them No.

If you are to thrive and succeed in telemarketing, the first rule you need to learn is *Don't Take No Personally*. Easy words to say, but not easy to hear.

I see a lot of people fail in telemarketing because they take rejection personally. They get rejected once and then they give up, giving into the excuse "*too much like hard work.*"

Anytime I have done telemarketing over the past 15 years, I have heard it time and time again. *No! Not Interested!* But, if you take a page from my book, you will rebuttal the prospect and ask; *Why are you not interested at this time*?

More often than not you will get one of the following replies, which I will explain further.

Let's look at the common reasons why a prospect will say Not Interested

1. *I Do Not Have Time*. Quite common a prospect does not have the time. Granted, in a lot of circumstances this can be seen as a brush-off, and no doubt it is. But, in this fast-paced world, there are those who genuinely do not have the time to get into an in-depth 20-minute conversation. Don't sweat this. Just place them on your call back list for another time. Chances are, unless the prospect has a memory for every call they have received, they won't remember who you are in 3 weeks or 3 months.

2. *Does not fit their budget*. This is also common. In today's marketing, businesses will allocate a certain amount of capital to their own marketing efforts. Unless they have a surplus of revenue they will not be looking at new ventures or additional expenses. On average, a business will review their earnings and profitability by the quarter. So again, this is worth reaching out to them at another time.

3. *Does Not Need*. What is the product or service you are trying to promote? If you are promoting auto detailing to an auto detailer, they are not going to buy your service! Know your market! A lot of businesses will buy databases based on generics and are not filtered properly. I see so many businesses make the mistake of purchasing data, only for some of the leads to fit into the category of "Competitor". They also may not have a genuine need for the service or product you are offering.

4. *Not Interested*! This is a flat-out Not Interested – period. Those types of calls you cannot do anything about, and sometimes the prospect will come across as rude

and unprofessional. Don't sweat it and again don't take it personal and bring yourself down to their level. I find that if you thank them for their time and wish them a good day, you will be better off for it and then move on to the next call. Call it good Karma, but it puts you in the right mind-set for the next call.

Of the four examples above, there is always an extended opportunity to revisit the prospect at another time. Whether that is in 3 weeks or 3 months. Recall and build a rapport with the prospect. You will find that building a rapport with the prospect will go a long way, and in the end, will get you that account! In some examples of my own telemarketing, I have worked an account for months with no traction whatsoever. Then one day, of the blue, the prospect is ready to deal. To date, these simple techniques have established me to be one of the few multi-national telemarketing experts around today.

While it is good to get personal with the prospect, it is always a fine line between personal and too personal. They do not want to hear about what is going on with the intricate details of your life. What they want to hear is about them. What do you know about their business? Did you take 2 minutes to do a google search on who they are and what they specialize in? You will find that this will go a long way.

The way to overcome objection in telemarketing is this sure-fire method that works like a charm. Just remind yourself that they prospect is saying No to the product or service offered. They are not saying *No* to you.

I have seen it time and time again where I have started a project and been shot down in flames more times than I care to remember. It is true that getting the first sale/meeting is always the hardest. That is so true, but the same can be said for anything in life. The thing is, what do you want to achieve as a telemarketer? Are you doing it to fill in time or are you in it to make a career of it?

If you want to achieve anything in life, you need to know how to handle rejection. Rejection is the killer of one's self-esteem, but what I learned is this simple fact: Switch off and focus on what needs to be done. Do the job, and if someone says no, that is no big deal.

Gene Kranz, lead flight director for Mission Control, said it best when he announced to the ground crew in Houston as Apollo 13 approached the critical earth-to-moon decision loop: "*Failure is not an option*"

Take this mind-set and you will certainly get a lot further in your career, whether you are in telemarketing for the short term or long haul.

If you need to, take a quick break, get up, walk around, get some coffee then get back into it. Having a good mind-set will set you for the next call.

If you have trouble dealing with rejection more, I suggest reading Dale Carnegie's book *How To Win Friends And Influence People*.

Remember this simple lesson in the art of dealing with rejection:

Don't take It Personally.

Chapter Five –

Traditional Marketing For Today

What works in today's modern world? As I explained in the Foreword of this book, using an online CRM and "googling" information about a company was as remote as home computers were back in the 1970's.

Back in the early 1990's, unless a business had their own data, it was commonplace for data companies to "sell" lists of residential and business listings. Quite often that data would be incorrect as it was gathered by using the current records from the Yellow and White Pages, and by the time it was put onto CD's, marketed and sold, the data would be at least 6 months old and inaccurate.

Many business owners I worked with in the early days purchased lists from companies such as OzOnDisc. And as far as I recall, that was one of the most reliable sources in Australia to purchase from. Times have certainly changed since the early days.

Today, unless you are a well known corporation, if you own a business in the average city of more than 100,000 people, it is unlikely that prospects will even know you exist. So what does work in today's ever changing market?

Internet: Since the boom of the Internet back in the late 1990's, the world wide web has exploded with more websites than what there are people. With more than 3,000 new websites are being created daily, and more than 6 Million new users every month[9], you need to keep up with the latest trends.

According to Internet Research[10], there were 186,727,854 active websites on the Internet in December 2008, and a staggering 31.5 million new websites added during 2008.

Quite a far cry from 1995 when the amount of websites totaled a mere 18,957[11].

If you own a SME in North America, you may be asking what do these figures have to do with me? Rightly so, in North America[12] where the population is an estimated 338 million people and 250 million users, the trend has grown at an average of 132.5% since the year 2000.

What that means for your business is that in order to stay in business, you need to keep up to date with the latest trends and the ever continuing way business is done in the modern world.

Long gone are the days when you could do business with the Joneses and have a customer for life. Today, in our fast-paced world people expect instant results, and more and more people are using search engines such as Yahoo and Google to find businesses in their area over Yellow Pages. Especially the Now generation where

---

[9] http://comunitadigitali.tumblr.com/post/91862952/with-an-estimated-3-000-new-websites-created-daily

[10] http://royal.pingdom.com/2009/01/22/internet-2008-in-numbers/

[11] http://news.bbc.co.uk/1/hi/sci/tech/1738496.stm

[12] http://www.internetworldstats.com/stats14.htm

teenagers and those in their early to mid 20's are tech-savvy and can whiz around the internet without blinking an eyelid.

I have heard it so often lately from businesses in Canada and the UK are suffering because of their *Old School* practices, and the thing is they want to penetrate the market – their local market – but their methods of reaching out are no longer effective unless they have a gimmick or a huge marketing budget.

One client in the UK I worked with came up with a novel approach of having a polar bear as their mascot for their removal business. As a test, they had someone dress up in a polar bear outfit and walk along the main roads, carrying their sign, close to where their office is located in North London. Apparently that worked as people saw the bear and associated the bear with the business.

Gimmicks can work for some product brands, whether it is Toucan Sam on the box of Kellogg's Fruit Loops or Chester Cheetah on the bag of Frito Lay's Cheetos. Sometimes gimmicks in marketing are good, but if they just don't fit with your product or service in a way that makes sense, they may be better left out.

If gimmicks do not fit your business, how do you reach an ever changing audience?

Advertising in the newspaper can be a cost effective way to reach out to businesses in your area, but also the market penetration is significantly lower than what it used to be, given these days that 99% of people you know will read local news on the internet rather than their local newspaper.

Radio and TV advertising can work, if you are catered for a specific time slot, but, if you are a small business, chances are that the cost of advertising on such mediums will far outweigh the revenue you will see, unless you have a product or service that is new, innovative and everyone will buy.

So how do you penetrate the market without breaking your budget? It is true that while having your own Dotcom has advantages, and will give you exposure to your local and regional market over time (with proper SEO marketing), more and more businesses are relying on the service of telemarketing. Telemarketing has proven time and time again to be a cost effective medium of penetrating the local or regional market far more rapidly than newspaper and internet advertising.

At one time, the cost of running a small call center once ran into the hundreds or thousands every month, given the scenario that everyone used a traditional phone-line to make calls, and unless they had an unlimited call plan with their telephone service provider, those call costs would be charged on a per minute basis and by the end of the month the phone bill would be in the thousands of dollars, depending on how many phone lines a small business had.

Enter Modern technology! These days, more and more businesses that are looking at starting a telemarketing campaign opting to use Broadband for their telemarketing, or in simple terms Voip.

Voip – Voice Over IP – allows a person to call other people's landline, cell phone or PC for next to nothing. Voip providers such as Skype, VoipCheap offer discounted rates and packages for PC users to dial an unlimited amount of numbers in any given month. Currently, Skype offers users an unlimited amount of calls for $12.95USD per month.

For those considering launching a small telemarketing project in-house, it is advisable that you familiarize yourself with Broadband packages and run with Voip. Your IT specialist will know how to advise you on this.

Voip is easy to setup and requires little skill. Most computers will come complete with an internal modem and sound drivers. All you need is a headset with microphone, Voip downloaded and installed and you are off and running!

There are some businesses that will try telemarketing, and after a week if they do not see any results they will give up and stick to other methods. But to those businesses I will say that it is not the telemarketing that failed, but the delivery. Quite often a business will launch a telemarketing project, and if they do not see immediate results, they will put it down to that telemarketing does not work. But in all honesty, what was done to try and make the project successful? Did you spend time training the telemarketer in the product or service offered or did you give them a script that you wrote while in the bathroom and expect the telemarketer to make sense of the gibberish they were handed along with a copy of the Yellow Pages that was dated 2006?

Some businesses, believe it or not, will hand the telemarketer a script that makes no sense, give them an outdated yellow pages and expect the telemarketer to know what to do from there, just because they are a "telemarketer". Again, in the history of bad ideas, this is a bad idea.

Just because someone who applies for the telemarketing position you have does not necessarily mean that they have experience in telemarketing or worse yet, knowledge of what your business does.

If you want a successful campaign, your telemarketer is your best weapon in penetrating the marketplace.

Let me ask you this; when you started in the business you are in, did you start your business not knowing anything about what your business will do or offer, or did you have experience in the industry you are now operating in, along with a formidable business plan behind you?

Unless you're Homer Simpson who once started a Dotcom business and had no idea what "an internet is", you would say that you did your research first and calculated what needed to be done.

The same applies for a telemarketing campaign. You don't give a telemarketer a script and expect them to know what your business does. They are not mind-readers as you would like to think they are.

Your telemarketer is your frontline, and the first point of introduction to what your business does. If you want your project to have a successful telemarketing run, then run the project properly from day one. If you give your telemarketer no real sales training and no script developing, other businesses will assume that you know nothing about business. The bad impression will not only be on the telemarketer for not knowing what they are talking about, but it will reflect on your business that you have no idea what your own business is about.

Just as a telemarketer needs to know their script, you as a business owner are expected to provide the correct material and product knowledge to your telemarketing team.

I see many businesses that try and launch with telemarketing but have no idea what telemarketing is about. I once spoke to a business that was considering taking on Yellow pages Online. Now, while they offered a unique service that would rival the online Yellow pages, they really had no idea about recruiting, training, skill sets, script development, and really nothing else for that matter. Even though they themselves had degrees in business management, when it came to telemarketing, they were going into it like a blind person.

Bottom line is if you want a telemarketing project to work, you need to know what telemarketing is about. It is a lot more than sticking someone on the phone and telling them to call everyone in the phone directory.

Whatever your goal is, telemarketing will definitely go hand-in-hand with your current marketing efforts and can greatly increase market awareness in the products or services you offer.

Traditional marketing serves a purpose, don't get me wrong. But the days are long gone when you can deliver flyers to people's home and wait for the phone to ring. Same applies for advertising in print media. Not everyone will read your ad, and those who do, unless they have an immediate need for what you offer, you could be waiting a long time for the customer to call.

Now, there will be those in business who have a database of existing customers, which is great. You have the base, now what do you do? If you have no web presence, chances are you won't be emailing your customer base anytime soon.

It is likely that your customers will have email, so as a business owner, you need to as well. Most businesses will already be using MYOB as part of their accounting software. So take the next step and get Internet savvy. The internet is not complex to figure out the basics, neither is setting up an email account.

Emailing your customer base is a great way to keep them up to date with what is going on in your business, or serves as a reminder that you are still in business.

You may say, "yeah but Chris, I have my repeat customers that come back a few times a year, so I'm all set."

Not true. Depending on the type of business you run, your customers need to be up to date. If you run a dental or doctors surgery you can use telemarketing and email to call on your existing customers and advise them of regular check-ups.

If you run a church, you can use telemarketing to reach out to new people in the community.

If you run an auto dealership, you can call customers to let them know of any referral programs or specials you have going on. (This works well with auto dealers, as you can go in with the pitch of: "*Mr. Jones, you purchased an SUV from our sales manager, Troy back in May 2008. We wanted to let you know of the deals we have going on with trade-ins so we wanted to know if you or someone you know is in the market for a new vehicle.*")

Telemarketing and Email is best effective way to penetrate whatever market you specialize in, and as I said above, goes hand-in-hand with what you are doing now.

Chapter Six –

Time Management: How To Balance Work & Personal Time

What is Time Management? Time management refers to a range of skills, tools, and techniques used to manage time when accomplishing specific tasks, projects and goals. These encompass a wide scope of activities, and include planning, allocating, setting goals, delegation, analysis of time spent, monitoring, organizing, scheduling, and prioritizing.

Organizing and prioritizing may be the two most important time management tip skills for successful people managing very busy activity schedules.

Time management skills can help you make the most effective, efficient use of your time. A good time manager is not necessarily the person who gets the most done. Rather, the good time manager is a person who knows the activities that contribute most to his or her long-term life development.

In any call center you are given an objective by your employer or team leader. In the average work day, you plan, prioritize, and set your own goals; whether those goals are 1 sale an hour or 1 sale a day. Your mindset is focused on the tasks at hand and you use your time effectively to meet those objectives.

Likewise, personal time management skills are essential skills for effective people. People who use these techniques routinely are the highest achievers in all walks of life. If you use these skills well, then you will be able to function exceptionally well, even under intense pressure.

Many people spend their days in a frenzy of activity, but achieve very little, because they're not concentrating their effort on the things that matter the most.

Organize and Prioritize

A typical time management tip would be that time management only has to do with making up a good "to do" list and following through. Right? Not really. This tip has a lot more to do with what we are NOT doing rather that what we ARE doing.

Good Time Management requires that we get what we "have to" get done but, more importantly, what we "want to" get done.

This requires balancing our lives in all of life's Vital Areas: Health, Family, Financial, Intellectual, Social, Professional, and Spiritual. If we are out of balance on one it is going to adversely impact on the other areas of our life. This is where we organize and prioritize.

Prioritize - I start most days with a "to do" list! I am the first to admit that I am not very organized when left to my own devices. If I don't have a set plan for the day I will get sidetracked and I end up doing everything else except what I really needed to get done in the first place. Categorizing my tasks by priorities eliminates a lot of wasted time. If you always start with the number one priority on the list and work your way down to the least, you will be accomplishing the most important tasks for yourself and your business.

That list should include what we are NOT doing, i.e. exercising, spending time with loved ones. Those who know me best can testify that in times past I was the typical workaholic. It was nothing for me to work 16 or 18 hours a day, sleep for a few hours then do the same thing all over again the next day, 7 days a week, 52 weeks a year. I continued that same routine for several years. I worked through the weekends, public holidays, annual holidays. I thought that I could make the most of the time I had to accomplish everything that needed (or so I thought needed) to be done, whether it was developing new scripts, database management, new prospects lists for the coming year, analyzing the past year productivity growth, further training and development coaching, or whatever else I thought about back in those days that was strictly business-related. My mindset was to meet all the priorities in that day, then start the same routine the next day.

In turn, my diet suffered as I lived on vast quantities of coffee and I ate whenever it suited, usually once a day or sometimes once every other day. I admit, eating and recreation was not considered a priority to me in those days, and I never took a vacation. Truth be told, I can remember that I worked so much that I took a two day vacation once in 4 years! And because I was so sold out to what I was doing (mainly freelance at that stage), my mind was primarily still on work, although I was meant to be taking time off!

Needless to say, although I found that I had maximized the most of my time in working like it was going out of fashion, the other areas of my life suffered greatly. Personal, Health, Social, Family, Spiritual. It took quite some time for me to discover the balance between all those things and start over. Through many mistakes I came to realize that the tools for increasing productivity there lied in a complete well rounded lifestyle.

Me Time! Remember this time management tip - take a minimum of one hour a day for yourself. A good friend once told me, "Take time for you and reward yourself." Not many people understand what this means, and if you ask people on the street how they spend "Me Time" they will answer going shopping, going out with friends, dining out with a partner, etc. Although those things are good as a pastime, they would not fit exactly into the category of Me Time. Me Time is all about you. Not your family or your friends. It is about taking an hour a day for yourself to do something you enjoy.

Whether it's taking a bath, going for a walk, going to a spa, or leisurely reading, make time every day for yourself. You will be amazed at how much more productive you will be when you return to work.

Lunch time! Do you stay at work - you don't want to miss a customer, or pay someone else to work through the lunch hour! It's like the parent that never gets a baby sitter. You will be more appreciative of your business and more productive if you take breaks and get completely away from your work station.

The person who takes work with them on their vacation and calls the office every day, never really had a vacation. Breaks and vacations are for the purpose of reviving you.

* * * *

Now although these things may be different than what you would experience in your regular 9 to 5 job in the call center, you can still apply these tips to maximize your efforts. Take 5 minutes every hour to refresh your mind. That works wonders, especially since you are sat at a computer for hours on end.

Before you start your day, organize. Organize your work day. Set a list of Priorities you want (or need) to get done. Maximize your efforts by applying the Time Management tips shared in this chapter.

By applying these simple skills you can optimize your effort to ensure that you concentrate as much of your time and energy as possible on the high payoff tasks.

This ensures that you achieve the greatest benefit possible with the limited amount of time available to you.

Remember: *Organize, Prioritize, Maximize.*

Chapter Seven –

So You Want To Work From Home

If you are a stay home mom or someone who enjoys phone conversations, then entering the telemarketing world can be your best option to earn limitless income.

There is a definite advantage of working from home. No commute in traffic, less stress, familiarity with your environment and if you have Time Management skills, it allows you to successfully balance home life with work life.

Since the Work At Home idea caught on some years ago, businesses are opting to hire freelancers to do telemarketing. From small and medium enterprises to billion dollar companies, telephone marketing still tops as among one of the most effective ways to promote products and services.

Businesses see Freelance Telemarketers as a fast means to get the word out about their product or service, and while it can be said that a majority of the larger business have an online training period before they set the telemarketer loose on the project, quite often small businesses do not have the same necessary skills or time to manage or train telemarketers.

In a recent [13] article, it is said that in the UK 1 in 8 people now work from home. While this statistic is across the board and not primarily in the telemarketing scope, there are more and more telemarketers who are choosing to work from home. Why? Because working from home allows the telemarketer to fit their home and family life around their regular work time. This is especially the case with those who have young children.

In the traditional workplace, there is a Golden Rule in business – *Don't bring your problems to work*. The same can be said for those who want to work from home, whether you are a company employee who works a certain amount of days from home or you are a freelancer trying to make extra income in telemarketing. In order to maximize your productivity, you need to be disciplined in order to work from home.

Now while working from home has advantages, not everyone is suited for working in this capacity. Working from home takes dedication, discipline, and essentially, time management skills.

While there are advantages for the employer to hire Freelance Telemarketers; there are also the negative aspects such as high retention rate, unwillingness to work, no supervision, lack of ethics and moral by freelance consultants.

Before I explain the benefits, I will explain the obvious; the negatives about Freelance Telemarketers.

---

[13] http://www.itpro.co.uk/196206/one-in-eight-work-now-from-home

More and more, freelance telemarketers are becoming idle and fail to follow simple company guidelines. A colleague that I have worked with on several occasions said to me last year, "*Chris I don't know what is becoming of America. People we hire to work from home are not working at all and then they expect to be paid.*"

This statement, although disheartening, is also true. There is a definite lack of Moral and Work Ethic in the case of 90% of all work at home telemarketers. But, this is just not in the United States. The same lack of work ethics are evident in the UK, and Australasia.

One client I worked with in the UK said to me, "*It is so hard to find anyone reliable these days. I just don't know what to do. My pipeline depends on sales, and for the life of me it is becoming almost impossible to hire diligent people.*"

The telemarketing industry is not the only industry to suffer. There is a definite rise of Lack Of Work Ethics in all sectors in the United States. More and more people are expecting an easy pay at the end of the week for very minimal effort. I see it all the time, from those who try and hire managers to those who try and hire home telemarketers. In the process, businesses suffer in the long run because of it.

Although the same cannot be said for the very small minority of those who do actually work, I have personally seen a steady decline in the ethics and moral of Work At Home Telemarketers over the years. In the present world which we live, there's a lot of people out there who feel as if they shouldn't have to work hard in order to be a success. But the *old-school laws* are just as dominant today as they were 20 years ago; *If you want to be successful, you have to work hard to be successful. Success is not something that will be handed to you because you want to sleep in or don't feel like going to work.*

I have seen instances with colleagues where a person worked 4 days in 10 because of one excuse or another, and then they expected to be paid for two weeks work. Needless to say they were paid for the days they *did* bother to drag themselves to work!

As an example of seeing just how moral has declined with work at home telemarketers, I posted a project on Guru.com for a project that I had with a client in Canada. The project was very simple. Cold Call business, tell them about the company and try and set an appointment. What we asked telemarketers to do was at the end of the business day was automatically upload their call stats and appointments for us to review.

Sound easy? Well to anyone who has experience in telemarketing it would be easy. The first week I saw 8 people apply for the position. Of those 8 I started 6 immediately, including two off-shore call centers (one in Pakistan and the other in the Philippines).

The first 3 days saw these 5 results (exactly as the messages were posted on a private discussion board):

Ch from Atlanta stated: *I downloaded and printed off the database as that is easier for me to work from. Do I need to upload the report?* – That part was already mentioned clearly on the project.

Lisa from KY stated: *Here is the appointment. It is for February 2010 as they need someone to do cleaning for the next Olympic games. Go see this person in February 2010.* – I am not joking. This person tried to pass off an appointment for 10 months in advance! She further added, *To ask for the data to be uploaded is unrealistic and to be frank I don't work for such demands.*

A. who runs a call center in the Philippines stated – *Why are we meant to upload the report and appointments?*

Bill from PA stated – *My g/f was in an accident so I couldn't work today.* The second day he said this: *I have thought about it and I really don't want to do this job.* (This was after he was awarded the project on Guru.)

Another person stated – *Thanks but I have decided that I don't work for such unrealistic requirements.*

The above examples are not the first time employers have had bad results from freelancers. The decline in Moral and Ethics is becoming worse each year.

For one reason or another the diligence and ethic has been thrown out the window for the hope of getting an easy paycheck.

If you are still reading this, it shows you have not thrown this book in the trash. If you are one of those who currently are a freelance telemarketer (or work at home telemarketer), before you go forming your opinion ask yourself this question; Have you truly fulfilled the requirements asked of you by your employer? Now I don't mean what you *think* those expectations are, but I mean the expectations outlined by the employer.

Chances are, if you are offended by the above statements and examples, you most likely have not followed the simplicity of what employers are looking for and ask. If you agree with what I have said, then you are either an employer or one of the few who actually do have work ethics.

While it does seem that the negatives outweigh the positives, there is a definite advantage of hiring freelance telemarketers.

First and foremost is that when you hire a good team, you can be rest assured that your productivity levels will increase; your overheads will remain at a minimal; and you don't have to spend a lot of time training staff.

Freelance telemarketers can be a cost effective way for you to reach your target audience in less time than it would take to hire and train someone in-house. A good telemarketer is worth their weight in gold, so if you have a good freelance team, make sure you have the added bonuses and incentives to reward them for the hard work they do put in.

* * * *

So what does it *really* take to be a *work at home telemarketer*?

As a telemarketer working from home, you primarily need a quiet area where you can exchange a smooth conversation with your potential clients and most essentially a computer with a microphone headset and Voip such as Skype installed on your PC. I would recommend that you have Microsoft XP Home Edition or higher on your computer or laptop. Second, and most importantly, is knowledge in using applications such as Web-based email, MS Excel and MS Word. If you are not familiar on how to use these applications, then it is recommended you learn the basics.

If you use Dial-up, change your plan to DSL/Broadband and get rid of your home phone line. These days you can use Voip which is far more economical than the cost of using a home phone.

Most telemarketers earn a minimum wage or on a commission basis. Your job as a telemarketer will entail generation and qualifying of leads (potential clients), setting appointments, phone sales, updating the database, trade show follow-up, research, up-selling and prospecting. Your network of contacts from various fields as healthcare, hospitality and tourism, commerce, education and health & beauty will come in handy in this kind of job.

Employers will give you the option to work part-time or full-time. Initially, your skills will be tested by the company on Day One. Your performance over the trial period will determine whether the company sees value in the services you render as a freelancer, or whether they will trial someone else.

If you value work, and want to earn a regular paycheck then it is recommended that you put in the work to get the rewards. A lot of employers will offer a bonus structure on sales or appointments set. Of those, a majority will also offer a base hourly. If you find such employer, impress them with what you can do, rather than what you *won't* do.

To put this in another way: If you are on the singles scene, when you go out on a date, do you put on your best appearance for your date or do you go to the date dressed in your pajamas?

Unless it is a fancy dress party, you will dress to impress your date and you will show them the better side to your nature. (or as I call it, *The Best Behavior Stage*). As you would agree, no one likes to date someone who dresses like they haven't seen the inside of a shower for the last month, so naturally you will look your best and be charming as you can be.

To put it another way. When you work for someone from their office, do you arrive at work dressed neat and tidy, and follow the company guidelines and do your best to meet their expectations, or do you arrive to work in your nightwear, smelling of beer with your hair looking like it hasn't seen a comb for weeks, and sleep at your workstation all day?

Just as you would work in a normal office environment, the same is expected from you working from home. But before you can assume that you will work from home, you do need to impress those who employ you.

The most important thing you need to be aware of is that you are not doing the employer any favors by working for them. The employer chose YOU for one reason or another. Be thankful for that opportunity they have given you and treat them with the same courtesy you would expect them – or anyone else for that matter – to give to you.

Impress the Employer and You Will Remain Employed.

Chapter Eight –

Modern Scams

With worldwide unemployment the highest it has been since the great Depression, more and more people are flooding the internet job boards in the endeavor to find reputable employment offers.

With the explosion of the internet era, there are dozens – even hundreds and thousands – of work at home scams. You see them every day with titles such as "*Earn $1000 this week!*" and "*Last Year I earned $100,000 by working from home*", and "*Earn $500 this week by stuffing envelopes*".

Such ads you will see all the time on directories such as Gumtree and Craigslist and other online web directories that have little or no moderation. These headlines often attract the naïve by offering a get-rich-quick promise and these are headlines – offers - that you should be aware of.

If you are someone looking to work from home, any reputable employer will not ask you for a fee to work from home. If you come across an offer such as that, it is a scam, plain and simple, and all you will get in return is a loss of your cash.

These scams are operated in the same way a Nigerian scam operated. You send them your details, they will respond with a detailed email (typically these emails are generic), and with a link where you can purchase the information on where to apply for the job.

If you have been one of those unfortunate enough to fall into that trap, then sad to say it is unlikely you will be able to do anything about it.

So with all the scams around on the internet, how do you know what offers are real and what are not?

The best place to source the most reliable jobs online are such websites as Guru.com, Monster.com, Seek.co.uk (and its affiliate sites: seek.co.nz, and seek.com.au), HotJobs, and CareerBuilder.com.

These five websites are content moderated and before any project or job is posted, it is first reviewed by the website moderator and approved or denied, depending on what content is posted in the offer.

Sites such as Monster, Seek, CareerBuilder and HotJobs typically charge the employer a fee for posting job offers, which ranges from $165 (Seek), to $419 (CareerBuilder) for one posting.

While the cost to employers can be in the hundreds of dollars for a single job posting for little or no applicants, it also serves a purpose in that the amount of scam job offers would be minimal or non-existent.

With the sites mentioned above, the job is normally posted for a period of 30 days, which, in comparison to traditional print, the cost is more effective, targeting a wider audience, as candidates from other regions or countries can view the job offer and apply respectively.

While these sites have the benefit of less scam job offers, the wave of poorly regulated job sites are the ones you, as a candidate, need to be aware of. The sites I am about to explain, although endeavor to serve a purpose, you will find that there are more scam offers on these job sites than anywhere else.

GetAFreelancer – GetAFreelancer (and its European sister site, EUFreelance), was started in 2004 and claim that they are one of the top players in the online freelance industry. (EUFreelancer is reported to be owned by a company in Singapore, and not many details are known about this site). However, while there is a free trial for employers to post legitimate job offers, quite often, the quality of freelancers is very questionable, such in the case of someone who hired two freelancers to work on a promotion project, and of those two "*experts*", (one based in India and the other based in Irvine, CA), the one in India tried to use the promotion for their own scam and the other tried to steal the rights to the owner's idea. For the efforts, the employer was charged $180 in fees, which in turn, took weeks to get a refund, so it was told.

Scammers targeting unsuspecting freelancers and employers are rampant on these two sites, and for both employers and freelancers, there are more reputable sites than GetAFreelancer and EUFreelancer.

* * * *

One of the most popular websites is without a doubt, Craigslist.

Craigslist is a centralized network of online communities, featuring free online classified advertisements – with sections devoted to jobs, housing, personals, for sale, services, community, gigs, résumés, and discussion forums.

Craigslist's sole source of revenue is paid job ads in select cities – $75 per ad for the San Francisco Bay Area; $25 per ad for New York, Los Angeles, San Diego, Boston, Seattle, Washington D.C., Chicago, and Portland, Oregon.

However, although Craigslist serves a great purpose in allowing employers to post job opportunities to nearly every region of the United States, Craigslist has also experienced a mass of controversies and illegal activities by its[14] users during its operations.

---

[14] http://en.wikipedia.org/wiki/Craigslist_controversies_and_illegal_activities_by_users

While it can be said that with the changes that are apparent on Craigslist, there is still a mass of scam job offers rampant. The easy way to identify such offers as the ones that boast unrealistic earnings, those that have a link embedded on their job posting (Such as in an offer that boasts: High Income Potential), and more often than not, the same job is posted in several regions of the United States, Canada, Australasia and the UK. Those types of job offers you should stay away from as not only are such offers unrealistic, but quite often ask you to pay them a fee to start. (Please note, that although there will not be any fee listed on the advertisement initially, if you fill in the online forms their link goes to, it is at that point when you will be asked to pay a *registration* fee, or you will get an email requesting that in order to complete registration, there is a fee involved).

So what type of jobs can I find on Craigslist? Certainly there are reputable jobs on Craigslist. 9 times out of 10, those job offers require someone to work from their office, and the work-at-home offers are few and far between, with more and more businesses downsizing or going out of business.

If you prefer to search Craigslist, search in multiple cities in the categories *sales / biz dev*, and *marketing / pr / ad* . Those are the categories where you will find any freelance telemarketing job offers. Granted, your search will take some time, if you choose to search every city in America and Canada, but if you repeat your search once or twice a week, your time can be spent less in finding real offers. On average, there would be 5 to 10 work from home offers that are legitimate.

* * * *

Another up and coming website is *Gumtree.co.uk*.

While similar to Craigslist, Gumtree is a fast growing network of free online classifieds and community websites. It is the UK's biggest website for local community classifieds and one of the top 20 websites in the UK. Local sites exist for Australia, Hong Kong, Ireland, New Zealand, Poland, Singapore, South Africa, the UK and the USA; although many are under the Kijiji and Slando brand.

While they do not have nearly as many job offers posted on their job boards, for those in the UK and Australasian markets, they are very competitive in the market and a recent search shows that in the UK and Australasia, there are more legitimate job postings than other generic job boards in the same market.

Finally, there is *Guru.com*. [15]Guru.com is a freelance marketplace. It allows companies to find freelance workers for commissioned work.

---

15 http://en.wikipedia.org/wiki/Guru.com

While the cost for Employers is free of charge, there are membership fees associated for Freelancers.[16] Memberships offered are the basic free membership to that of a Guru Vendor for $130 per quarter, plus associated fees on Project Fees, which run at 5% for Guru and Guru VENDORS or 10% if one is a basic member.

Although many people who are registered on this site opt for the basic service, it does allow for Employers to find candidates by industry experience. The same applies for Freelancers searching for projects. The advantage of using Guru for Freelancers is not only can you set up Notification Emails in the categories you want to work, but there is content moderation on all job offers that are posted. So in the case of the employment scams, on Guru you will not find many – if at all any.

* * * *

With the mainstream sites such as Monster.com, Seek.co.uk, HotJobs, and CareerBuilder.com, as a freelancer you can post your Resume for free and then search the areas of employment you are interested in pursuing.

While HotJobs does require you to be a registered user of Yahoo, you can search the advanced job boards by filtering by location and industry, while CareerBuilder's advanced search allows you to filter up to 3 categories and 3 locations.

* * * *

If you are a job seeker, in order to maximize your earning and visibility potential, it would be worth your while to register on Monster.com, Seek, HotJobs, CareerBuilder and Guru.com. Yes, it will take time to complete all requirements that each site asks, but if you are serious about finding work, then you will put in the time to get it done.

You are not going to get offers straight away, but what Employers do look for is History. Work History. The more details you have posted on your Freelancer Profile (Guru), or Resume Profile, you will have more chances of actually being hired by a reputable employer.

Once your Resume profile is built, don't sit there and wonder why you are not getting offers. Building a Resume profile is one thing, then you need to spend time in hunting down job offers.

If you spend an hour or two a day searching for work and submitting your resume, you will find work.

Search the boards on Monster, Seek, HotJobs, CareerBuilder, Guru and finally Craigslist.

---

[16] http://www.guru.com/about_guru.cfm?tab=how

If you are serious about finding employment, that is where you will find the jobs. Not by sitting and waiting.

Ask yourself this: *If I can't be bothered in creating a good resume, then why would an employer be interested in hiring me?*

A Great Resume Will Attract The Employer.

Chapter Nine –

Business Making Business

Outsourcing has become a viable and affordable means to outsource call center projects to developing call centers in countries such as India, Pakistan, China, Singapore and the Philippines.

Being cost-effective for many companies – such as banks, government departments, and most other places where you call a toll free customer service number – means finding a solution that otherwise fits the growing demands of a corporation. Outsourcing an Inbound project to call centers offshore means little or no overheads, no ongoing recruiting and lastly, the project gets fulfilled.

While this has proven to be viable for a lot of Inbound campaigns, with the promise of cheap labor as low as $2US an hour in some call centers, outsourcing an Outbound project does not always prove profitable, especially if you own a business in North America, the UK or Australasia, and you are targeting prospects in your region.

The willingness and work ethic of some call centers in developing countries is strong, and it is true that if you get a good call center offshore the results can be profitable, but more often than not, leads – your leads – are wasted because a majority of call center staff in developing countries speak English as a second or third language, and the message conveyed to your prospect is often lost, and in turn, you have lost a potential customer.

If you are a business what options do you have in the ever changing world? Hire an in-house staff? Outsource to a developing country or take a chance of Work At Home people, who actually may not work from home. There are advantages and disadvantages to all three options.

Hiring In-House – While the option may be there for Small to Medium sized businesses may be to hire in-house, there are advantages and disadvantages to the options. On one aspect, you have the cost of advertising in your local newspapers, as well as online mediums such as Monster, HotJobs etc. Along with that the time and money spent paying your recruiter to filter out the candidates, the time taken to train, additional expenses spent in computers, phone lines, taxes, 401k's, and not to forget the additional day to day expenses associated with running a business are increased with more staff.

Now while there seems to be definite gloom for the employer, there are the advantages to hiring in-house telemarketers. Your staff work the hours you require, their production can be monitored, and at the end of the day, you get the results you need a lot more rapidly than any other option.

Home Telemarketers - While it can be said that there are reliable freelancers on the marketplace, more often than not, you would do a lot better by starting with an in-house program in conjunction with any outsourcing you may want to run as a test operation.

As I explained in the chapter of *So you Want To Work From Home*, there is a major downside to hiring Home telemarketers. The work ethic of a majority of individuals has gone downhill rapidly to the point where they expect an easy paycheck for very little effort. It is the case of "*You pay me for producing no results, and if I feel like submitting a report, I will*". Seriously folks that is the state of play in today's world. I ran the same project twice on Guru, one offering $8 an hour, then the same project at $17.50 an hour, both generated the same results. No matter what country you try and find freelancers on through such Freelancing sites, you will come across the undependable and the unethical more often than what you will find the ones who have the ethic to drag themselves out of bed.

Offshore Call Centers – Call centers in developing countries in India, Pakistan, and the Philippines offer an eagerness that has not been seen in America for the last decade. Project Managers in such countries are all too eager to run a project, based on your requirements. Quite often, you will find new call centers starting in these developing countries so fast that in years to come, these developing countries will lead the world in the call center industry. Their work ethic and moral is high, they follow direction well, and in some countries, the cost associated with using agents you can find for as low as $2US an hour per agent.

While you are not going to come across too many call centers that will offer workers at $2US per hour, the medium is around $5US per hour per agent. Still a lot more economical than utilizing call centers in North America. With the premise of cheap labor and high work ethics, this option is not flowing with Milk and Honey.

In 99% of all call centers in developing countries, English is the second or third language, and often, not spoken very well. While we are all accustomed to the Americanisms we use in everyday life, such phrases and complex sentences elude the would-be telemarketer, and if you listen to one of their recordings, you will see how even the simplest script can and is a stumbling block, even for a tele-agent who has some years experience in that call center.

I first started dealing with call centers offshore back in 2002, when I gave several call centers in India the opportunity to generate appointments for a copier dealership in California. Even back then, the simple script we provided was lost in the delivery, and those call centers ended up burning more valuable leads than what could be salvaged.

In 2005 I revisited such call centers, this time for a different project. The project was simple. Generate leads for a software company. Again I got the same results as the previous time. Once again I tried call centers in Pakistan and India. This time I trialed them on a very easy project. Janitorial Appointment Setting.

Results? Same as before. They had no idea how to set appointments. After 2005 I vowed never to deal with call centers in developing countries again. However, in 2009 I decided to put those previous negative experiences behind me and try again.

I sourced the resources of 3 call centers. One in the Philippines, one in Pakistan and one in India. The project was as it was before. Cold call businesses and set appointments for a commercial cleaning company. Once again, as it was in 2005, and as it was in 2002, the call centers burned leads. They could not understand the simple terminologies Americans and Canadians used, and as a result, the leads – valuable leads – were wasted.

While you may not have experienced the same, more and more businesses who have trialed call centers in developing countries for Outbound Cold Calling have met the same results. A colleague I worked with some years ago, he experienced the same results over and over again, no matter what call center in India he trialed. All of them had bad use of the English language and could not generate results. His last dealing with them resulted in him telling me, "*Chris. I have had enough of those guys. They have no clue what it means to run a campaign. They need to stick to what they do know how to do. Inbound.*"

Sad to say, but also true.

The options for business looking for a solution seem hard at best, with the lack of work moral by Work At Home telemarketers and offshore Call Centers that have no understanding of the complexities of the English language. It does seem that in order to run a profitable campaign your best option is to hire a team of in-house staff, train them in your office, and monitor their progress.

While the overheads are there for running an in-house project, the results would be what you want.

Not every business owner will agree, but you may want to try a test for yourself to see the results, and compare for yourself which is better.

In-house, Freelancers, or Offshore.

Chapter Ten –

Getting The Most For Your Buck

The bottom line in any call center project is you want results. When you start a call center it is in your business plan to succeed and have the best agents working for you. But finding the best agents is not an easy process. There is the time taken to place advertisements, the costs associated with advertising, recruiting personnel, interview and screening process, then hiring the individual(s). telemarketing has a high industry turn-over. In fact, one of the highest in any industry. As an employer what can you do to have less turnover and loyal staff?

Over the years I have had the pleasure of working in some great call centers that were managed and owned by great people. Some of which in my home city of Sydney Australia.

For an industry that has a high turnover, a call center I worked for some time ago had very little – in fact no – turnover whatsoever. Why? because they believed in what they were doing; had high moral; rewarded their staff, and most importantly, treated their agents like they were people.

Sound strange? Not so. Let me explain.

In today's age, it is becoming more and more common to see employees as nothing more than an employee. Not as a member of a team or a valuable contributor to the business, but a number, a docket in the payroll.

In my experience such people have low morale and almost dread going to work. There is no life in the call center, and the only thing such employees are looking forward to is the end of the week when they get their paycheck.

Believe me, I have seen it time and time again. Call centers than ran like sweat shops.

However, on the other end of the spectrum, I have seen call centers thrive. Why? because their managers and leaders played an active part in the daily operations of the call center. Not just as someone who listened to calls at random, but they actually got on the phone to makes calls themselves. Team playing. Although it may be seen as a foreign concept to have your team leaders making calls along with the rest of the team, you would be surprised in what results that will being, especially if one of your telemarketers turns around and generates more sales for the day than the team leader!

It will give them a sense of purpose, victory and improves their self-esteem.

Daily bonuses, prizes. These all part an intricate part of rewarding your team. One call center I worked at had on offer a large HDTV as the prize for the month. Now, every time a telemarketer got a lead, they would get a ticket and put it in the barrel and at the end of the month the owners of the business would draw a ticket at random and whoever name was on the ticket got the prize!

Morale! Goal Setting! Incentives!

While HDTV's may not be in your budget, you can surely offer your team incentives and prizes to get results to improve.

Although it will not necessarily mean that you will have fewer turnovers, it will mean that at the end of the day you will have employees that will like coming to work.

I remember some years ago, when I worked with a call center in Columbus Ohio. The task of the telemarketer was to sell printing labels to businesses. Now while they had a large call center with close to 100 telemarketers, the morale was not the same as the call center in Sydney.

Why? Although the team leaders did their best to encourage the staff, there was a definite separation of class between managers and agents. As part of company policy, it was almost taboo for a call center agent to associate with a manager during breaks, and as a result, this effected the productivity of a lot of agents, so much so that I saw many agents quit after a few days, and other after a few weeks.

Although a separation of class is standard in some call centers, the point I am making is this: the call center in Ohio saw a huge turnover rate, while the one in Sydney didn't lose one.

Why? What is because of the building looked nicer? No. Was it because there were more pretty girls at the Sydney call center? No. Better pay? No.

Simply put, team leaders were on the same playing field as the rest of the crew. Although the team leaders were team leaders, and got a higher salary, they were also on the phone doing exactly what everyone else was. Making calls. Dialing, making appointments, hitting goals.

Your team leaders need to be on the same page as the rest of your crew. Yes, incentives can be fun, but if you want fewer turnovers, use the example of the call center in Sydney.

Chapter Eleven –

Telemarketing Tips from Successful Telemarketers

This chapter I would like you to consider each of the following telemarketing tips to improve your sales and bottom-line profits. These tips work, as they have been used by me and other Professionals in the Industry. You want maximum profitability?

Apply these tips for 30 days and analyze the results for yourself.

- ✓ Don't sound like a telemarketer!

- ✓ You have just a few seconds to make a good initial impression on the phone. Your careful preparation for the call can increase your chances of having a conversation with a prospect rather than hearing that familiar dial tone.

- ✓ Always be courteous and professional. Remember, you're a sales professional who just happens to use the phone to sell.

- ✓ Be sincere and believe in the product/service you are selling. People will sense insincerity on the phone even though they can't see your facial expressions or other non-verbal communication clues such as hand gestures, head nods and body posture.

- ✓ Keep your work area neat - it'll keep you focused and organized.

- ✓ Dress like a sales professional even if your prospects will never see you.

- ✓ Keep a mirror handy so you can check to see if you're smiling during calls.

- ✓ Don't practice on prospects with a few warm-up calls at the beginning of the day or week. Role play with someone if you need to, or just talk out loud in an imaginary conversation to warm up.

- ✓ Meeting annual goals requires setting and meeting daily goals. (Time Management). Record your progress on a daily basis.

- ✓ Keep records of the contacts you make for future reference. Note dates for follow-up.

- ✓ Keep track of your success rate in getting through to the decision maker or closing a sale. This will help you identify and correct any weaknesses in your strategy or approach.

- ✓ Use your prime selling time - the hours your prospects are most easily reached by phone and are the most receptive-for selling activities only. (Experience will quickly let you know when your prospects are most receptive!) Conduct homework, research, planning or other administrative activities at other times.

✓ Use past experiences to help you prepare for and react to current situations. For example, if you continually meet the same objection to buying what you're offering, brainstorm all the different ways you might meet this objection so you'll be prepared the next time it pops up.

✓ Develop a script for the call to keep you on track but never read directly from it. Write the script as you talk. That way, when you vary from the script, your words and phrases will be consistent. As you write your script remember all these great telemarketing tips.

✓ Consider using introductory or follow-up letters, product fliers or other marketing materials.

✓ Use other "communication" tools as necessary to support your telephone sales, including cellular phones, fax machines, hands-free headsets, email, etc. For example, part of your selling process may be to offer prospects a product information sheet by fax or email.

✓ End calls quickly, but politely, when it becomes evident that a prospect is either not qualified for your product (you're selling a dating service and the prospect is married) or the prospect is not going to buy. Your time on the phone is precious. Spend it selling!

✓ In addition we encourage you to focus your discussion with your prospective client on what they need and what they want.

✓ DO NOT try to convince them of what they need or want. Instead, ask probing questions and let them tell you. Once you know what they need, they you can suggest the perfect product match.

There you have it. Apply these tips as part of your calling program and you can gauge the differences you will see.

About The Writer

My journey into the world of telemarketing didn't happen by choice. It was back in 1994, when I was living in Brisbane, Australia, and at the time I had recently left the Nursing Industry. I was looking for a change in life, and quite by accident, I was offered a job working part time for an insurance company in the northern suburbs of Brisbane.

Although I had no idea what telemarketing was about back then, I was eager to learn, and more importantly I was looking for an easy paycheck.

Up until that point I had never done a day of telemarketing in my life. Although I was naïve to the industry, and thought nothing more of the business, I was blessed with a natural ability to generate results.

After learning the initial script that was handed to me by Paul, I memorized it and picked up the phone. Making that call, the first call, changed who I was and set me on a road that would define me as to who I am today.

In 1994, my journey started with calling home owners, talking to them about life insurance and education plans and then setting up an appointment for one of the insurance guys to visit them.

The company I worked for had 7 insurance sales people on deck. My job was to keep them busy, and so I did. In any given week I was setting anywhere between 60 to 100 appointments a week, every week. Back then I was titled the "*one man sales force*".

Telemarketing and I have come a long way since 1994. In that time I have successfully (and personally) generated close to $500 Million USD in sales and proposals for clients worldwide. I have worked with startup companies through to multi-million dollar corporations in the US, Canada, Australasia, and the UK.

I have been dubbed as one of the few "Multi-national telemarketing expert's" who has an in-depth understanding of the industry.

When it comes to telemarketing, I can help you create a viable campaign from an idea to launch, and show you how to recruit the best talent in the industry, whether you want to run a small project or a 50-seat subscription campaign.

If your business needs help in your project, whether it is scripting, training, recruiting, call center start-up, or if you want to rally your team to new levels in production, contact the writer at:

Chris Jackson

leadsnz@yahoo.com

Cell: +7-937-175-1972

LaVergne, TN USA
19 August 2010
193956LV00001B/87/P